Stewie Scraps

and the

Space Racer

Written by Sheila M Blackburn
and illustrated by Leighton Noyes

 Brilliant Publications

Brilliant Publications
www.brilliantpublications.co.uk

Sales Office
BEBC (Brilliant Publications)
Albion Close, Parkstone, Poole, Dorset, BH12 3LL, UK
Tel: 01202 712910
Fax: 0845 1309300
e-mail: brilliant@bebc.co.uk

Editorial Office
Unit 10, Sparrow Hall Farm
Edlesborough
Dunstable, Bedfordshire, LU6 2ES, UK
Tel: 01525 222292
e-mail: info@brilliantpublications.co.uk

The name 'Brilliant Publications' and the logo are registered trade marks.

Written by Sheila M Blackburn.
Cover illustration and inside illustrations by Leighton Noyes.

ISBN numbers:

Stewie Scraps and the …	Space Racer	978-1-903853-84-9
	Easy Rider	978-1-903853-85-6
	Giant Joggers	978-1-903853-86-3
	Star Rocket	978-1-903853-87-0
	Trolley Cart	978-1-903853-88-7
	Super Sleigh	978-1-903853-89-4

Set of 6 books ISBN 978-1-903853-90-0
6 sets of 6 books ISBN 978-1-903853-91-7

First printed by Dardedze Holography in Latvia in 2008
10 9 8 7 6 5 4 3 2 1

The right of Sheila Blackburn to be identified as the author of this work has been asserted by herself in accordance with the Copyright, Designs and Patents Act 1988.

If you would like further information on any of our other titles, or to request a catalogue, please visit our website www.brilliantpublications.co.uk

Contents

For Hazel, a very special friend, and with thanks and love to Tom.

A huge thank you "to everyone at Brilliant Publications and especially Priscilla Hannaford".

Grand plans

It was late September. Stewie Scraps had been in Mr Melling's class for just a few weeks. He didn't like it much.

"You'll be all grown up now you've gone into the Juniors," said Grandpa. But Stewie knew it wasn't true.

Grandpa had called Stewie a "little scrap of a thing" when he was a newborn, and the name had sort of stuck.

So did his size.

And no matter what Grandpa said about being grown up, he was still the same little scraggly Stewie Scraps for the big lads to tease:

It didn't help that Stewie's dad, JJ, owned the untidiest junk shop in town.

If Stewie ever said anything back to the Year 6 gang, he was in for it.

6

They followed him round the playground when the teacher wasn't looking, shouting:

"Sn-a-ppy Scraps

Sn-a-ppy Scraps.

Can't take the pressure

Sn-a-ppy Scraps!"

It wasn't much better in class either.

Stewie hated Maths. He liked reading and writing even less. If Mr Melling asked a question, Stewie never put up his hand to answer. He left that to others.

If Mr Melling asked Stewie a question, it was a disaster.

"Me, Sir? Don't know, Sir."

Then Mr Melling (or Smelling, as the kids called him behind his back) would sigh and tut and ask one of the clever kids.

   8

It made Stewie feel even worse.

In fact, Stewie spent all week wishing that Friday afternoon would come. This was because Mr Melling did something called "Art and Craft" on Friday afternoon. It was the only lesson that Stewie willingly took part in.

One particular Friday afternoon, Stewie became unusually excited. The class began work on a new space project, and Stewie knew exactly what he wanted to design.

He set to work straight away on the plans for a new spaceship. Mr Melling stopped by Stewie's table and asked him about it.

"It's my idea of life on Earth in the future, Sir," answered Stewie. "Planet Earth will be overrun by mutants if we don't take action now, Sir."

It was a long speech for Stewie Scraps. Mr Melling could not ignore it.

"What sort of action, lad?"

"We must find new planets, Sir," Stewie explained. "New places to live on, Sir."

Mr Melling was trying hard to understand.

"But do we have the technology?" he asked the class generally.

   10

"I'm working on it, Sir," said Stewie Scraps. "And I've got everything that I need to make it at home.

There will be an inter-galactic, robotic braking device on the landing pod, Sir," went on Stewie Scraps (as if it was the most natural thing in the world).

"Of course!" said Mr Melling, totally baffled, "I should have known."

Stewie Scraps then proceeded to paint his spacecraft design.

It was a funny mixture of black, purple and burnt yellowy-gold.

Mr Melling watched closely. He was particularly impressed. Stewie's design was full of imagination and ideas that Stewie actually wanted to talk about. So Mr Melling decided to make a request.

"Stewie?" he enquired. "Please may we keep your spacecraft design in school over the weekend? I would like to show it to everyone in Assembly on Monday."

Stewie looked horrified.

"But, Sir – I need to take it home as my prototype," he said.

"Your prototype?" repeated Mr Melling slowly.

"Yes, Sir. It needs modifying. But I reckon I've just about covered all the details for my real spacecraft … ."

"You have a real spacecraft, Stewie?" Mr Melling asked.

Somebody laughed.

"I do, Sir," Stewie replied, seriously. "And I need this model to work from at home – please, Sir."

"Very well," said Mr Melling. "But take care of it, Stewie. I'd like you to bring it back to show in our Assembly."

"I will, Sir," said Stewie Scraps, "just as long as I get back in time."

Mission control

Straight after school, Stewie sneaked in through the gate to the backyard hoping everyone would be too busy in the shop to notice him.

Bad luck! His Mum was out there, trying to give Bric-a-brac, the dog, a brushing.

"Hi, Mum!"

"Hello, dearie," Flo sang out as she tugged at the brush in Bric-a-brac's thick coat. "What you got there, our Stewie?"

Bric-a-brac groaned.

"It's a spacecraft design," Stewie explained. "A prototype."

"A protototo-what, dearie?"

"A prototype — something I can work from when I make the real spacecraft tonight," Stewie told her.

Flo chuckled and the great folds of her flowery overall rippled and waved.

"Go on with you, our Stewie!" she said and went on with her brushing.

Bric-a-brac groaned again and rolled onto her back.

Stewie hurried off to the shed at the end of the yard. He pulled open the rickety door that creaked on its hinges and went inside.

A musty smell and deep gloom reached out to him. He moved forward and tugged at the dangling flex. A dim bulb came on in the cobweb-laced roof above him.

"Are you there, Bugzy?"

There was a scuffling sound and the little white rat appeared from the open door of his cage. Stewie bent down and picked him up.

"Hi, Bugs. Look what I made at school."

Stewie held the model spacecraft for the little rat to sniff.

"It's not a patch on the real thing, of course – but it got me thinking ... just a few changes here and there – eh, Bugs?"

The rat twitched its whiskers and sniffed at Stewie's inter-galactic egg-box model.

"Stew-ie!! – Want some tea?"

It was Poppy, Stewie's big sister. Her voice floated through the ether, like a battery-powered chicken.

Stewie put down the spacecraft design and went to the shed door, stroking Bugzy.

Poppy was in the yard. Her purple- and orange-streaked hair stood out a mile off.

"Oh, yuk – that disgusting rat!" she shuddered as Stewie came blinking into the light.

"Want some tea, Stewie? I'll do pickle butties."

"Ugh! I'll get my own later, thanks," Stewie said.

"You off out, then?" asked Stewie.

"Yeah – with Mikey."

She sounded pleased, and a guy with burgundy, super-glued spikes put his head around the gate at the back of the yard and grinned.

"They make a good pair," Stewie laughed to himself.

Stewie turned back into the shed, closed the door and pulled the old curtain cover off the workbench. It was time to work on his very own spacecraft – The Space Racer.

"Good job nobody else ever comes in here, Bugzy," he said, quietly.

He set the rat down on an old oil drum.

"I'll get the things I need from the shop tomorrow ... . It's always busy on a Saturday. Nobody'll notice me in there rooting about."

Bugs twitched his little pink nose, sat down and began to wash his whiskers. Stewie moved round the workbench in the dim light.

"We just need to collect a few extra bits for the landing gear ... that's all ... and then – all systems go – tomorrow night! That's the plan, Bugs!"

Busy day

Saturday was a miserable, wet day where leaves came hurtling into the yard behind the shop on a chilly wind.

"It's a lazy wind, this one," Grandpa said, when he came back with the newspaper. "Too lazy to go round – it cuts right through you."

He winked at Stewie and went to find another woolly waistcoat to wear.

"Lazy wind or not – I've got a load of stuff to collect this morning from Hope Street," said JJ, Stewie's dad, at breakfast time. "Some nice bits and bobs – so I'll need you, Clint, and you, too, Stewie."

And that was that. Stewie knew better than to argue. He knew the score.

Clint was Stewie's older brother and Poppy's twin – but he was ten minutes younger than she was, which he hated.

Clint would help JJ with the carrying and loading.

Stewie's job was to chat to the sellers and take their minds off things. JJ always got a better deal when Stewie was around chatting.

It meant less time on the Space Racer this morning, but there'd be more chance to lose himself in the shop later on …

… and more stock to choose from.

Stewie worked hard all morning.

He chatted about planet Earth and mutants and the need to explore other planets.

The man with all the bits and bobs was getting a little tired of Stewie's chattering.

"I'm planning an expedition myself," Stewie told the man.

"Yes, of course you are!" the man said, without really thinking.

"I hope to survey life forms in other galaxies ... . There may well be other planets worth exploring – in case we have to move off Earth one day ... ."

"You're thinking of moving off planet Earth?" the man asked. He looked hopeful. "When will this be?"

"Just as soon as the landing gear's fixed on the Space Racer!" Stewie told him and took an armful of bits and bobs to JJ and Clint at the van.

Stewie Scraps had bread and jam for his Saturday dinner. He sat behind the wobbly counter in JJ's shop and dripped jam onto the greasy floor.

Flo rubbed at the red stickiness with the sole of her shoe.

"You watch out for our best carpet, dearie!" she laughed and gave him a playful cuff.

30

JJ and Clint were in the back, picking at things from the morning's load.

"Want a hand, Dad?" Stewie asked when he'd licked the last of the jam off his fingers.

"OK, Scraps!" JJ called. "See if you can find a place for these."

Stewie was happy to trot to and fro with the bits and bobs that JJ unpacked, following JJ's directions to the shelves where they were to be piled or put in boxes. He didn't mind a bit.

On his way back and forth, he noticed quite a few other useful-looking bits and bobs that might come in handy – things that JJ had probably collected while Stewie was at school that week.

It was time well spent.

Besides, the afternoon got busy, as he hoped it would.

Flo and JJ were serving and sorting for hours. Clint went off on his motorbike to see a mate. Poppy was at her Saturday job, filling shelves in the local supermarket. Bric-a-brac was busy having an afternoon snooze and Cast-off the cat was occupied in the shop, pouncing on customers.

So, nobody paid any attention to Stewie Scraps … and that was exactly how he wanted it to be.

By the time the September sun had sunk down behind the flats off Bold Street, Stewie Scraps was back in the shed at the bottom of JJ's yard.

Bugzy climbed onto the old oil drum to watch.

Stewie uncovered the workings of the spacecraft. He walked round it and frowned.

Then, he took up a screwdriver and a hammer and set to work.

   34

First, he pulled some of the side panels off the Racer, then he hammered, then he added some of the different parts from his afternoon pickings in JJ's shop.

"It's not really stealing, you know, Bugzy," Stewie explained, with bits of metal sticking out of his mouth. "I'm just borrowing this stuff, you see. I'll probably have to take the whole thing to bits when the expedition's over – so everything'll end up back in the shop, where it came from … . There! That should do it."

With one last tap of his hammer, Stewie Scraps was finished.

35

He stood back to admire the finished Racer. Bugzy ran up his arm, sat on his shoulder and nibbled at his ear.

"No – not tonight, Bugzy. Bit of a problem tonight, see. I forgot – it's Saturday night – and I don't want to be off on a space mission and missing out on fish and chips for tea!"

Stewie Scraps pulled the old cover over the finished racer and put Bugzy back in his cage. Then he was gone across the yard, following the smell of fish and chips that Poppy was unpacking on the kitchen table.

   36

We have lift-off

Sunday morning was crisp and dry under a clear blue sky. Stewie woke to the smell of bacon frying.

"Sunday!" he said to himself and pulled on his jeans and an old, patched jumper.

"Can I take my bacon buttie down to the shed?" he asked.

Flo sipped at her fourth mug of tea and nodded.

"OK dearie," she said. "Mind how you go."

JJ's was open all day Sunday, just the same as the rest of the week. It was an important shopping day for all the DIY people and for those whose cars needed mending, or whose taps wouldn't stop dripping.

Grandpa always helped in the shop on Sundays – and Poppy and Clint would be off doing their own thing. Stewie could have an adventure all on his own.

Stewie stepped inside the shed.

"Hi, Bugs," he called and opened the rat's cage. Bugzy stretched and pattered out into the dust on the wooden floor.

Stewie watched him. That was when he caught sight of the shiny metal nut that had rolled a little track in the dust and now lay near the old oil drum.

"That's part of my cybo-bolt, Bugzy! What's that doing there?"

Stewie snatched up the nut, pulled the cover off the racer and climbed inside to fit the part somewhere under the command console ... .

That's when it all happened.

39

No sooner had Stewie fitted the nut and cybo-bolt in its correct place than there was a loud humming sound.

The humming got

LOUDER and

Then the humming became a

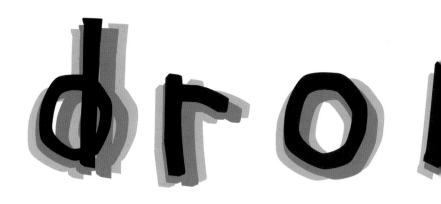

   40

And
the droning became a

roaring

and
the roaring became a great, great

BOOMING SOUND.

The Space Racer began to shake.

It
shook
and it
rattled
and it

shuddered.

42

It shook so much that Stewie was thrown back into the command seat. He just managed to jam his old cycling helmet on his head, grab Bugzy to haul him on board and pull at the brake lever, all at the same time.

Then, with an enormous

WHOOOOOSH

the Space Racer shot forward through the open shed door.

As soon as the Racer reached the clear light of day, Stewie tugged at the nose lever and the space racer rose

up and up and up.

It cleared the wheelie bin; it cleared the wall at the end of the yard; it cleared the High Street.

"Wow!" said Stewie Scraps.

He looked down at JJ's old van and some other trucks and cars that were fast becoming little specks far below him.

   44

"Hatch cover down!" Stewie commanded and at once found himself tightly packed inside his Space Racer with only Bugzy for company.

Stewie Scraps gulped.

A few whispy clouds sped up to him at an alarming rate.

"This is it, Bugzy. This is really it!" Stewie whispered and felt the Space Racer lurch into Over-Warp-Drive around him.

The clear blue sky swirled and twisted itself into deep blue, then dark blue, then total black.

Stewie peered ahead through his meteor-proof screen and blinked at the millions of stars that were winking right back at him.

For some time, Stewie and Bugs shot through outer space at a rate that was both very, very fast and very, very scary.

There wasn't time to do much more thinking about that sort of scary stuff, though, because now the Space Racer had changed direction. It seemed to be dropping down, like an extremely high lift might plummet to the ground. Stewie's eyes grew wide with a new fear – crashing.

Through the meteor-proof screen, Stewie saw the outline of a planet growing bigger and bigger.

Within seconds, he could make out sea and land masses. The Space Racer's engine note changed to a high-level whine and the ground rushed up at them.

It was worse than the twister ride at the Autumn Fair – pure thrills and terror.

Bugzy took cover under the command seat.

In the end, Stewie closed his eyes.

47

Strange new land

The Space Racer landed with a surprisingly soft thud.

Immediately, the command console panel gave an atmosphere read-out. It was safe!

UNSAFE | A BIT DODGY | SAFE

49

The meteor-proof screen lifted and Stewie Scraps found himself looking across a landscape that seemed shining and fresh. In some ways, it looked like Earth, with clear water and growing plants – yet on closer inspection, the whole view was shimmering with a silvery dust.

Stewie looked up. There was a strong brightness above him that shone onto the silvery dust and made it shine and shimmer.

It was beautiful. So beautiful.

"You can come out now, Bugzy," Stewie commanded. "It's perfectly safe and really, really beautiful."

The little white rat appeared from under the command seat, still shaking.

"This," said Stewie Scraps, "is exactly the sort of place we'll need when life on Earth is no longer possible. When Earth has been overrun by mutants, we can all come here instead."

He pulled himself to his feet and climbed out of the Space Racer. Bugzy chose to stay inside the Space Racer, nervously washing his whiskers.

Stewie's Space Racer had landed next to an enormous silvery-blue lake. Stewie made his way over to the shore, knelt down and cupped his hands to drink. The water tasted cool and quite sweet.

Stewie looked up, squinting in the brightness that bounced off the surface into his eyes.

He blinked, rubbed at his face, splashed it with water and looked up again.

Across the vast sheet of silvery-blue, two eyes — two huge, enormous, green eyes — were watching him. And they didn't look very friendly, or very pleased.

Stewie sat down by the shore with a bump. He shielded his eyes against the brightness.

Better to say something. To introduce himself.

"Hello! I'm Stewie Scraps. I'm JJ's son. He's the guy with the shop on the High Street – but you wouldn't know that, would you? Not stuck out here … ."

He was jabbering now.

He would have said more, but suddenly the brightness faded as if someone was dimming a light. Stewie gasped.

The eyes were now glowing a deep red in the thickening gloom – and they seemed to be coming right across the lake, straight at him!

"Wh… wh… who are you?"

Stewie's voice sounded very little now that the brightness had faded. He felt suddenly small.

"You're scaring me – who are you?" he whispered hoarsely.

The eyes came closer, blazing red, very angry looking.

"I'm not alone, you know," Stewie whimpered. "There are others on my spacecraft."

The eyes, deep red and glaring right into him, hovered directly over him. A deep, rich voice with anger rippling under the surface, seemed to come from the eyes, somehow.

"What do you want?"

"Me? … Oh … you know … just looking."

It was the sort of thing people said when they came into JJ's shop.

The eyes glowed as red as the hot wood at the heart of a bonfire.

"Looking for what?"

Stewie was terrified.

"I ... I came in peace," he said in a little voice. "Honestly — I didn't mean any harm.

Th-there's only me and a cowardly rat. We came to see if there's anywhere better than planet Earth."

"Why?"

"J-just in case we ever needed to get away ... ." Stewie hoped it sounded more convincing than it felt.

"SO ... !"

Boomed the eye-voice.

56

"You think you can come here and ruin this planet, like you have your own?"

"But I d-don't want to spoil anything … ."

"Then take a look!"

Stewie nervously looked around then back over his shoulder.

In the dim light he could see the Space Racer … and the path that he had taken to walk to the lake. He suddenly noticed that it was no longer fresh and shining as before.

It was black and withered.

"Did … did I do that?"

"You did. It's the same sort of thoughtless damage that your people do to your own planet. It is not wanted here. YOU are not wanted here."

Stewie looked back at the eyes. They now looked even angrier and seemed to hover above him, moving even closer. Stewie leaned back until he was almost flat on the ground.

Then, just as it seemed that the eyes were about to swallow him up completely, they flashed away over his head.

At the same time, there was a deafening roar, as if all the Space Racer's rockets were firing on overdrive all at once.

Stewie squeezed his eyes tight shut.

Then a hand ruffled his hair.

"You all right there, Stewie lad?" asked Grandpa, looking round the shed at the many parts of the now-broken space rocket. Cast-off was sitting on top of a pile of metal where the Space Racer had once been.

Stewie looked embarrassed.

"Pity about this," said Grandpa, picking up the frazzled nose cone. "I suspect that the heat on re-entry into the Earth's atmosphere did this," he added. "Never mind, you still have the design to take into school on Monday."

Stewie moved closer to look at the nose cone. It did look very burned and battered. He looked up, wondering what to say.

But Grandpa just winked. Then arm-in-arm, Grandpa and Stewie walked out of the shed.

The End

Stewie's big brother Clint is always out with his friends on motorbikes.

"Oh, Wow! Come and look at this, Stewie!" calls Clint. It is a beautiful glistening red and chrome motorbike with long steering rods and long cow-horn handlebars!

Later that night, Stewie secretly flicks through Clint's bike magazines until he finds a picture of *that* bike. Then he does something really daring – he rips the page out of Clint's magazine.

Find out how Stewie builds his own bike and what happens on the Easy Rider's first outing.

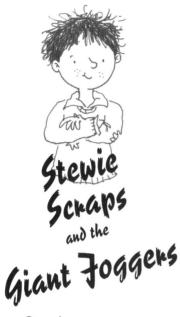

Stewie Scraps and the Giant Joggers

Sheila M Blackburn

Stewie goes on an overnight school trip. It is his first time away from home and his first time in the countryside. His head is full of ideas for making this and making that.

Back at home, there's a surprise birthday party for Grandpa and a welcome home for Stewie.

Grandpa's present is a new pair of slippers. "Could you get me a new pair of legs to go with them?" he jokes.

In the dead of night Stewie sits bolt upright. He knows exactly what his next design is going to be.

Find out what Stewie builds and why he ends up in a mass of grass, leaves and twigs in the shed!

Stewie Scraps and the Trolley Cart

Sheila M Blackburn

Alfie Battersby, just about the cleverest and richest boy in Mr Melling's class, hands Stewie an invitation to his karting-party.

"Wow!"

Stewie is on Alfie's team at the karting track. He tries to remember everything he's been shown but it isn't as easy as he expects – and he isn't the only one having problems!

It is all over far too quickly.

Back at the flat, Stewie heads for the shed as soon as he can. "Got to get it all down before I forget." But his new design doesn't go according to plan. Find out what goes wrong and how Grandpa comes to the rescue.

Stewie Scraps
and the
Super Sleigh

Sheila M Blackburn

"Merry Christmas" reads a battered plastic sign in JJ's dusty shop window.

A new boy starts in Stewie's class and they soon become friends. Then Stewie realizes that since Miles came along, he hasn't come up with any new designs.

"That's it," he exclaims. "I've had an idea at last … . Perfect. Everything I need is here … . Look at my design," he tells Bugzy, his pet rat. "The Stewie Scraps Super Sleigh … bet you can't wait!"

Stewie sits on the driver's seat of the sleigh … but nothing happens. Why won't it go anywhere? Where will the Christmas Magic come from?

Stewie Scraps and the Star Rocket

Sheila M Blackburn

"You still like fireworks, don't you, Stewie?"

On Friday 5th November, Grandpa's local pub is holding a fireworks party for charity. "You could come with me." Grandpa suggests.

Stewie thinks about it. Maybe it would help refine his Super Star Rocket design.

Stewie is spellbound by the firework display. He's never seen such big rockets before.

The next day, it takes only a couple of hours to find all the bits needed for his Super Star Rocket. But what will happen when Stewie tries to launch it?